CREATE WEALTH
using the
"Masturbation" Method

by Rose Palmer

Stop fretting...
Remember LIFE is
sexually transmitted!

Fact: The brain is
the largest sex organ.

*This is a fact that
we can use to our
own* **fiscal** *favor.*

~Rose Palmer

Table of Contents

Introduction

Wealth building is a serious topic. Most people would like to improve their wealth-building skill set. To that end, I'm using an analogy EVERYONE can relate to - let's be honest...

I'm using the analogy of self-pleasure merely to make a point about how **personal** a "path to prosperity" really is. This is not intended to teach people to pleasure themselves instead of go to work or anything silly like that - so relax. It's a tongue-in-cheek (or a tongue-in-somewhere) look at something we all naturally do.

**If the topic offends you,
please don't read any farther.**

If you are continuing to read, even knowing you'll be offended, I can't really help you. Just so you know - you won't be able to 'un-read' some of the really strikingly memorable descriptions you're going to read in this book.

All the same, I sincerely hope that I can help the others by giving them an interesting, new and humorous way to look at wealth consciousness. A way that they can keep thinking about - pleasantly several times a day.

Basically, this is the **'erotica'** version of a wealth-consciousness book.

Wealth is an
"Inside Job"

Yes, this is another one of those proverbial "how to get wealthier" conversations.

Are you tired of reading the same thing over and over again? How many of these lessons have you learned? It is my goal with this book to give you some new things to think about. However if you've already done some studying on the topic of wealth creation, you'll be able to understand these illustrations really well.

I really doubt this is your first time down the "prosperity" book path. But if it is, welcome - you'll have a great time going down this path with these tools as the first ones in your 'tool kit.'.

What's different about this approach?

Why should you care?

If you have you read lots of other books about abundance and wealth creation and are still frustrated with where you are in life, then it's definitely time to lighten things up! Have no fear, this is truly a serious wealth-building book, however, we're going to give the subject a really cool new **"stroke!"**

We're going to talk about the principles of attracting money, but use the analogy of masturbation to explain it. *Don't worry, I will never say that word again, because I think it is a little harsh, besides, there are so many other awesome euphemisms for it.*

Getting rich is all about mindset. It is an inside job. It is about self-worth and a ton of other "self" words - including self-gratification. No one else can help us get into a wealthy mindset. It is all about you - and only you!

Just like no one else can 'diet' for you or work out at the gym for you or get healthy for you, no one else can **"tussle your muscle"** for you and no one else can get you into the wealth-building mindset. You have to do all of those completely on your own.

Get Rid
of the Noise

First, I need to take all the noise out of your head. If anyone ever told you that you 'can't get rich' in this day and age, because the economy, or circumstances are against you, imagine telling them to go **"whack-themselves off"** for a moment, because you've got something you want to learn. Get their well-meaning, but totally destructive comments out of your head!

I'm going to assume that you are reading this book because you want to get to a comfortable or even affluent type of lifestyle and you're not there yet.

If I'm wrong about that, then hopefully there will still be some nuggets of good information for you here. If not, hopefully at least some entertaining things to think about.

If you'd like more money to be attracted into your experience, so that you can reach a greater expression of a lifestyle (that you might currently feel is beyond your means), let's get to work **"buttering your corn."**

The Parallels

I got the idea for this book while **"working out at the Y."** I was just about to reach a Tipping Point, that point (at least for women) where they know they are going to be successful and reach orgasm. Then the words of a wealth meditation I had been using went through my mind and I started to laugh.

The tipping point for women is just a sensation. It's one that most women know. After several minutes of **"sexercising,"** certain sensations begin to go from feeling very nice to feeling amazingly intense and suddenly you know that you're going to make it to climax.

For whatever reason, I realized that I was at a Tipping Point - or a point of no return - and I recalled the lesson from a great abundance teacher (who I'll paraphrase to preserve her anonymity in case she doesn't want to be associated with the topic of **"jerking off"**).

She said, "When you get your thoughts aligned and the financial manifestations are starting to become obvious, you will reach an obvious tipping point. After which, with far less work than you ever dreamed possible, abundance manifestations will begin to show up in your life."

When I had that realization, I remembered back to several times in my life when the money was flowing really well and there really was an Obvious Tipping Point and it happened without too much work on my part, especially once the momentum started to gather.

Once I made that comparison, I wondered if there were any others comparisons between creating wealth and **"Friction Therapy."** Guess what! There were tons of parallels. That is what the rest of this book is all about.

Meditation vs. "Yankin' the Yam"

Every single one of the wealth gurus out there will tell you that you should take some time with yourself and meditate, mostly to clear your head and focus your thoughts. Relatively few people actually take up the practice of meditation just by reading a book that says you should do it because it takes practice and discipline to do it. Many people are intimidated by the word, or possibly feel that it might conflict with their other spiritual beliefs. No matter your feelings on meditation, I can guarantee that at some point in time, have **"buffed the weasel."** That's taking some time with yourself...

Let's compare these two exercises.

❖ Meditation, you do alone. **"Beating Your Meat,"** you do alone.

❖ In either case, you don't want anything/anyone to interrupt you.

❖ Both meditation and **"diddling yourself"** have the same outcome - if successful, they both leave you unwound and more relaxed.

❖ In Meditation, your breathing becomes slower and deeper. **"Clapping with one hand"** also changes your breathing pattern for the better.

In abundance teachings, most of the good that comes from meditation is the release of resistance, not necessarily the refocusing of the thoughts (although if you can do that too - it's very good). So, in a very real way, taking time for yourself this way is your first steps toward a meditation practice. Don't tell your guru I said that... but I still bet he/she would agree - kinda.

The objective is to release resistance. You need to release resistance because when you hold something you'd like to manifest in your thoughts, many times you're not really imagining how nice it would be to have it (prosperous mentality), you're actually picturing where you are right now because you don't have what you want (lack mentality).

Most of us can't help it. It's hard not to focus on circumstances. But it is critical to focus on desired outcome instead.

Today's circumstances are an out-picturing of what you thought about yesterday. If you think the same thoughts you thought about yesterday, then tomorrow will be about the same as it is today. Hence, we are actually running around on a vicious circle that is a lot like a hamster wheel, when it has just felt like we were stuck. We're not stuck. We're running all the time. We're just running in circles looking back at yesterday hoping tomorrow will be better, but not changing anything significantly enough to make that happen.

To break that cycle - let's think about the future right now.

Let's anticipate all of the wonderful things that could happen, not work 'face' or overcome whatever situation you're in right now. Take a lesson in anticipation from **"spanking the monkey."** Rarely, do you say, I'm not there yet, I'm not there yet and quit. No, you know - with certainty - what the pleasurable outcome will be if you just keep at it. That is anticipation. You're thinking about the future, not the present. That is one of the reasons it works so well and feels so good.

When you are thinking about the future, it pulls you along to it. When you're mired in circumstances, they pull you back to the past where you blame yourself or others for the situation you're stuck in.

When you are thinking about the future, the anticipation builds and it gets more and more exciting. When you think about the past, it keeps you attached with a chain to that hamster wheel going nowhere.

As anticipation builds, things seem to happen faster and faster until... you're suddenly there. Success. You've just released all your resistance - and a bunch of endorphins too!

If you can't get into meditation, at first, don't worry, just go **"be your own best friend"** because many of the benefits are the same.

Do NOT snicker the next time someone suggests you meditate, you'll get me in trouble!

Working it

One of the things that wealth teachers profess is that most of the manifesting work takes place before you see any results. Which is also true when you're **"Gripping Your Dip."** 99% percent of the time, it is work before you reach the climax. It's pleasurable work, but it is work to get there. The actual climax (objective) doesn't really last all that long.

This has another parallel in a famous and very true saying, "Do what you love and the money will follow." Do what you love to do and something good is bound to happen... Don't snicker (out loud) when someone says that to you from here on out either!

Keeping Score

When you look at current results or 'keep score,' you're looking at the present - which is an out-picturing of yesterday's thoughts. If you stay in yesterday's thoughts today, you get today's same results tomorrow.

You wouldn't dig up a seed to see how far the roots have grown and replant it and expect that seed to keep growing normally. Of course not, you'd realize that would nearly kill it, and it would have to recover from that. Likewise, keeping a score sheet of your wealth building can't be done by looking at your bank account. You can't yield anything new there by looking at those numbers constantly. Your job is to do the work today that will yield results tomorrow.

You can't see tomorrow's deposits by looking at your online statement today. You can only be sure that those deposits are coming and work on anticipating the feeling of that. Many wealth-consciousness teachers advise you to print out your statement. White out the balance that is there and write or type in the balance you want to attract.

Then stare at that statement!

My father was an engineer and he tracked everything. There were charts for everything all the way back to my childhood and how much allowance he'd ever given me. So, I learned how to track circumstances. And I was really good at it.

I thought that if I could track circumstances in real-time, then I could immediately see trends, and react quickly to keep momentum going. Sounds good in theory, but it does not work in practice.

I built a system to have e-mails sent to me hourly if after automatically checking the program had detected any sales. So, when good something happened - usually hourly - I'd stop what I was doing and work to figure out what that alert was trying to tell me. This didn't gain me very much at all. The few times there was something tremendous happening, it was out of my control, so I couldn't make it bigger or better. I could just be distracted by it. Being distracted took me away from what I was doing, so ultimately, those great happenings, usually ended up causing setbacks, because of how I handled them.

If you feel the need to keep score or to track your progress, just be sure that you are also doing projections and seeing all the positive potential, not just 'what is' or it will do you more harm than good.

Keep your mind on the ultimate prize (the orgasm of the situation) and just do what you have to do to get there without taking too much stock of circumstances along the way.

Why there is a
1% vs. 99%

Do I dare say it? Money gives them a hard-on.

For most of us it seems, money is a struggle. Getting it, keeping it, having any left over after you pay your bills. Thinking of our job as our only 'source of supply.' That's where most of us fall down and that is why most of the 99% are the hard working people of society and the 1% gets to laugh all the way to the bank. They don't think of wealth building as a struggle - to them it's a game, it's fun. It's as fun as **"Cranking the Shank."** And that's as it should be.

Read the other prosperity guru's and listen to them talk about how we've all been fed a bunch of hooey all our lives about 'Having to work hard for an honest day's wage.' I don't want to go into that piece of this puzzle as in-depth as so many others have before me because I don't want you to think about your circumstances. I want you to get excited about your potential. So the way we look at 'working for money' vs. 'money working for us' is the paradigm shift that must happen here.

It's all in your head.

It's simply all in the way you look at it. If you could imagine that making money was as fun as **'fiddling with the ferret,'** you'd do it all the time - right? Well, that's the way it is with the 1%.

They've also released the fear and baggage that goes with making and keeping a lot of money.

They don't care about how much tax they're going to have to pay, they pay more in taxes than most people earn in a year, but that means they have all that much more still in their accounts. Don't fear the tax man, remember when you're wealthy is when you get all the tax breaks!

The 1% don't care about what other people think.

The 1% don't care about people trying to get it from them, the 1% have their ways of protecting their assets already established. You will too.

Do the Sparkle Phillips' (*Finding Your Fortune*) trick of imagining you've won the lottery and deciding who the first person is you're going to call. She goes much farther into that exercise. It's really eye-opening. It's also a very great way to visualize a bunch of money coming into your experience suddenly. So do it!

The 1% have thought enough about money that they have created solutions around all their anticipated problems. The 1% don't worry about the what-if's anymore, they focus on what's next. What-ifs don't create fear for them. The 1%ers just focus on what they need to do, not all the possible collateral problems.

So too, you have to start thinking of having a lot more money as something completely pleasurable, not something stressful. Just like with **"getting in touch with yourself,"** it's all good.

Don't Tell Anyone

This is critically important!

Do you announce when you're going to go do the **'Hand Dance?'** No, of course, not. You don't want to be teased, judged, scolded or otherwise distracted. You do this for yourself because you want/need to feel better.

Creating wealth or working on your abundance consciousness is the same thing. You don't tell anyone you're doing it - especially your parents, your friends or likely your significant other. Wealth-building talk makes them just as uncomfortable as if you were to announce to them you were about to go do the **'Jazzy Jerk.'**

Besides, you know as well as I do, that telling someone about something extremely personal always brings out the Advice Monster.

Your people will either tell you their personal horror story about money, or a story about someone they know - like you! It is the time when everyone decides to remind you of all the other things you've tried before in life and how well that turned out for you. Even though you can comfort yourself in the words of Edison*, getting reminded of other's opinions of your life is never pretty. So spare yourself the agony. Nothing good comes from it.

*'I have not *failed*. I've just found 10000 ways that won't work.'

The real reason they will try and talk you out of what you are intending to do is that they simply like the status quo. If you suddenly got a ton of money, things would change. It'd make them feel weird. They're not thinking about how good it would make you feel, only that things would change for them and since they wouldn't be able to control it (or you - because you'll be wealthy), it creates an 'Unknown.' Unknowns make people very uncomfortable. So they tend to do what they can to discourage you to keep their own status quo.

My advice:
Just don't tell them.

Just show up one day, and let your generosity show through. No one will try to talk you out of getting rich when you're picking up the tab. They'll slap you on the back and say, "Good for you... I always knew you could do it." Imagine that... I bet you can.

You don't need anyone else's permission to get wealthy. You don't need anyone's permission to get more fit, or to go on a diet. Working on your personal financial fitness is something you do for you. It's no one else's business.

Getting a wealth mindset is a very personal journey. You won't get approval from others. You won't get validation from others. You won't get help from others. You have to do it by yourself, for yourself and with yourself. Just like... well, you know.

Dream stealers don't consciously mean to be dream stealers, not really. But they still are quite effective at dashing dreams all the same. Don't give anyone access to your dream to damage. It's all yours. Protect it!

Just build your dream and once you do, let others enjoy it with you. Don't tell anyone - not because you're ashamed, but because you need to maintain your focus without their words running around in your head - innocently - or not -sabotaging your self-confidence.

When they ultimately ask you, "How'd you do it?" I dare you to tell them that you just got **'in touch with your Inner-Millionaire.'** (My apologies to Sparkle Phillips).

What's to Be Learned From Doing the Deed?

First, you get the idea that you'd like to **"Pump Your Power,"** likewise when wealth building, there is always also an idea. In the words of Ernest Holmes, "Ideas are God's gold coins." Everything starts with an idea.

Next, imagine the <u>best possible outcome</u>.

You are certain of the possibility of orgasm or climax when **"handling the goods."** You know you can do it, because you've done it before. So too, with wealth building. With the idea comes the possibilities. Imagine what that kind of "climax" looks like. The difference is the knowing of the outcome of orgasm because you've done the deed many times before. With wealth building, unless you've ever had enough money (all the way up to a major surplus) in the bank, and know how that feels, you have to anticipate that greatness that first time.

If this is your first time wealth building, there might be some uncertainty about the outcome. Work to erase that doubt, by visualizing (over and over) the successful outcome of your idea. As much as you can 'see yourself' being successful doing the 'ménage a moi,' can you see yourself being successful accomplishing this idea? Can you visualize your bank account's balance where you would like it? How much is that? How many individual deposits had to come into your bank to make that happen? Is it one mass deposit or a monthly/weekly/daily addition to your bank account? What does that look like on a piece of paper? Can you see it? Does that give you a hard-on or make you wet? Let it.

Don't read on until you've answered those questions. Really think about them. Don't think about what you'd have to do to get them, just think about the amounts of the deposits and what you could do with them.

You need to find a place you can be **'alone with your thoughts.'** You need to be able to plot, daydream, figure things and create the space for success. Where is that? Where can you work securely without fear of interruption or ridicule? Where can you go without the worry of the prying eyes from dream stealers? It doesn't have to be too far off the beaten path. Right now, I am working at my desk, just like I'd work on any project. But I have this master file on a place where I can work on it from my desk, cell phone or any laptop. So I've created a mobile/virtual space to work.

It took me 3 years to write my first book, because I wrote it in total secret. I just waited for the kids to go to bed and I worked on my computer instead of watched TV. I created the space I needed to do what I needed to do. If my husband had known I was writing a book, he'd have asked me about it, or been discouraging because it took me 3 years to write or possibly might have disapproved or wanted to me to make plot adjustments to please him. But I kept it secret from him and everyone else. That book spawned a business and between that book and the business I've been able to support myself and my family quite comfortably for 15 years now. And I expect to be able to do that and more for the rest of my life and then some. It all started with a secret.

Keeping it secret is what kept it on track. At least for me.

I shudder to think of what my life would be like now if I hadn't written that book when I did and how I did.

Find your time alone and do the prep work. There's a lot of massaging and rubbing to get things going when you're **"Dating the Rosy Palm"** but you knew that when you started. So, it's okay to do some work when you're changing the way you feel about money to be able to attract in more. As long as you can stay focused, you know it pay off in the end. So too, will the foundational work for your idea take time, yet pay off too. Do what you need to do so that you're ready when things really start to take off.

With anticipation building now, you're prepped and ready and working hard to make things happen. Success is within your grasp (literally). Now you've reached the proverbial "Tipping Point." This is where you know you are going to get the job done and you know it is going to be soooooooo goooooooooood.

Now that 90% of the manifesting work has already been done, and you have past the point of no return, so you can just relax and let nature take its course.

Wow, there you are. You did it.

You've just produced millions of something... even if it was just endorphins, you produced millions. Your neurons are snapping happily away and your resistance to everything has faded into the background. Your bliss is all that you know.

Milk this moment. Do everything you can right now to remember this moment. Burn it into your memory bank. What do you feel? What do you smell? What do you see? What do you hear? How fast is your heart beating? What parts of you are tingling? We are talking about seeing that money actually deposited in your bank - aren't we?

When you reach success in whatever you do, take a few extra seconds to milk the moment, so that you can bring it back into sense memory clearly and quickly. Over time, you'll find you can remember the good times so quickly and that will raise your personal sense of bliss as well. Raising your vibration (as Abraham Hicks defines it) will lead to more and more and better and better things happening in your experience.

But Seriously Folks...

First off, learning wealth consciousness does not equate to making money. This book is not instructing you to do the **"Knuckle Shuffle"** instead of go to any paying job you have.

Creating wealth consciousness is creating an atmosphere where wealth can be attracted to you. This might be a new idea that pays off - like writing a blog that becomes popular, or creating a viral video, writing a book or a screenplay or even just a good Squidoo lens. It might be gaining the confidence to go for that promotion or even winning the lottery. The point is not to worry about the how more money comes in, it is about creating the environment (and belief system) where it can show up. It is about giving enough attention to the subject of wealth consciousness that you'll recognize the opportunities when they do show up. It is about getting comfortable and releasing resistance to everything that has held you back in the past - most noticeably other people's opinions - or fear thereof.

There's enough examples of thousands of people who have had money miracles come into their lives as soon as they made a psychological shift to something more positive. That is my intent with this book, to teach you how to achieve that shift. Get your mind off what is, and on to the anticipation of something glorious. Just keep the end-game in mind, the 'how will I do it' will come to you in a moment of inspiration. **You don't have to have that first, you just have to have the desire/idea that you want it to come.**

So, the next time you're **"Cuming into your own,"** you just might think of a parallel or two in this book, snicker to yourself and remember when it's all said and done, that you just created millions of something... and with that knowing, that certainty of outcome - possibly you can apply that mindset to your own dreams.

Go for it!

A Note from the Author

I wanted a fun new way to look at the topic of wealth building. So many people take the subject so seriously, but I think we all need to lighten up a little.

If it is all about gratitude, loving life and just getting happy, what better parallel than describing an act that we all do, love to do and are grateful we can do?

This is a titillating topic and when you combine it with the topic of wealth building, the parallels are funny, and the images from the lessons really stick in your mind.

I know I'm being irreverent and even a bit crass, but so what. This book is intended to drive home a few really important points about how you personally can strike gold.